A JOURNEY OF SPIRITUAL DISCOVERY AND KNOWING GOD PERSONALLY

THE ESSENCE OF KNOWING GOD

PETER O. OLATUNBOSUN

COPYRIGHT PAGE

Title of the Book:

KNOWING GOD: A LIFE-CHANGING DISCOVERY

Author: PETER O. OLATUNBOSUN

Copyright © [2024]

ISBN 978 – 97 – 8 – 769796 - 2

Request for information on this title should be addressed to The Publisher:

Request for information on this title should be addressed to The Publisher:
petfav001@gmail.com
Abundance Media Incorporation

PREFACE

How do I know God? Is He knowable? Is it worthwhile to know Him? These questions, and more, will find be answered in this book. The devil, through his enticing and deceptive tactics, is relentlessly taking advantage of people, children of God inclusive. Many people are thus unable to identify him for who he is. He erodes their lives and controls them to his advantage. The relationship between God and man is compromised because of the activities of the devil. Having the correct knowledge of God is the panacea for this worrisome trend.

Taking the pains to know God is worth all the effort. It will enable better decision making, grant wisdom, and give victory over the devil. Over and above that, a warm and thriving relationship with God is cultivated in the process. The journey of knowing God is not an end in itself. It is a transformative journey that transcends our cerebral capabilities. It takes place in the heart and is a quest for intimacy with our maker.

> [19]"and to know the love of Christ that
> surpasses knowledge, that you may be filled
> with all the fullness of God."
>
> Ephesians 3:19

In the Bible, knowing God is equated to eternal life (John 17:3). This underscores the importance of developing a thriving relationship with God.

We know from Proverbs 9:10 that, 'The fear of the Lord is the beginning of wisdom'. True wisdom is found, not in the accumulation of knowledge alone, but in the acknowledgment of God as the source of it.

Knowing God: A Life-Changing Discovery, is an invitation to study the word of God, which carries the very essence of God himself, in a most intimate way. It is a beckoning into the warmth of spiritual intimacy, where we transition from mere acquaintances to intimate companions of God. It is in knowing God that we are known by Him, as His children. Personal encounters and divine revelations, when based on the word of God, are vehicles on which we travel to know God intimately.

We start our lives as babies, curious and eager to explore the world around us. Similarly, our spiritual journey starts with us as spiritual infants. As we grow older, we should prioritize knowing our creator and our place in the world He so lovingly created for us.

It is my earnest prayer that the quest to know God becomes an all-consuming passion. A failure to know God has consequences on our spiritual lives and the overall quality of it. Apostle Paul tells us the unfortunate situation of spiritually immature Christians.

> [1]"Brothers and sisters, I could not address you as people who live by the Spirit but as people who are still worldly—mere infants in Christ.[2]I gave you milk, not solid food, for you were not yet ready for it. Indeed, you are still not ready. [3]You are still worldly. For since there is jealousy and quarreling among you, are you not worldly? Are you not acting like mere humans?

1 Corinthians 3:1-3

Knowing God will help us to make the most of our time here. Journeying through the pages of this book, we will explore the essence of knowing God personally and experientially. We will be taken through the stages of spiritual growth, from childlike wonder to the fullness of sonship, discovering along the way, the profound truths hidden in the sacred scriptures. Each chapter will unveil a new facet of knowing God, inviting us to deepen our intimacy with Him.

This book will serve as a guiding light on your spiritual journey, illuminating your path to a deeper and more meaningful relationship with your creator. It will inspire you to seek God with all your heart, soul, and mind, and to experience the abundant life He affords those who know Him personally.

In His service,

Peter Olatunbosun

TABLE OF CONTENT

CHAPTER 1

THE PURSUIT OF INTIMATE KNOWLEDGE

An intimate knowledge of God is to be desired and pursued. It connotes a full understanding and recognition of God as the source of godly knowledge. Acquiring spiritual revelation and putting the same to practice are the delight of those who seek to be intimate with God. If we are not hungry for God, we will be unable to take those steps that will draw us closer to Him (James 4:8).

There are many knowledgeable people who are unable to apply spiritual principles to their lives. This is because natural knowledge is different from spiritual one. For instance, it is not uncommon to find that people who have succeeded in their careers and businesses unable to hold their marriages together. This is because it takes an intimate knowledge of God to make a Christian marriage work.

Intimacy with Him

God desires His children to pursue an intimate knowledge of Him. It is when we remain in close communion with God that we are transformed into His likeness. Only then can we go on to live the life He designed for us (Romans 12:1-3). God is deeply pained when His children are careless about their relationship with Him. On countless occasions, this caused His displeasure with the children of Israel. At a point, this was his opinion about them.

"3The ox knows its owner, and the donkey its
master's crib; but Israel does not know, my
people do not consider."4Alas, sinful nation, a
people laden with iniquity, a brood of evildoers,
Children who are corrupters! They have
forsaken the Lord, they have provoked to anger
The Holy One of Israel, they have turned away
backward.

Isaiah 1:3-4

These words remind us that, like the children of Israel, many neglect to seek an intimate relationship with God. On the contrary, they embrace the sinful way of life handed over to them. We, as the new Israelites, are expected to be more intentional about our relationship with our creator.

An intimate knowledge of God infuses us with courage and strength. This is especially important, going by the world turbulence we are experiencing now. Only those intimately acquainted with their source will stand the test of time.

The veil is rent

The veil represents a barricade into God's presence. It connotes blindness or unbelief, and a hindrance to perceiving the truth. The veil between God and humanity was torn from bottom to top (Mark 15:38). By so doing, God extended a direct invitation to intimate communion with us. No longer should we settle for second-hand relationships with God, through human intermediaries.

For seekers of an intimate knowledge of God, the days of running from pillar to post, seeking help from fake prophets are over. We are called to approach God boldly through the saving blood of Jesus Christ.

> [19]"Therefore, brethren, having boldness to enter the Holiest by the blood of Jesus, [20] by a new and living way which He consecrated for us, through the veil, that is, His flesh, [21] and having a High Priest over the house of God, [22] let us draw near with a true heart in full assurance of faith, having our hearts sprinkled from an evil conscience and our bodies washed with pure water. [23] Let us hold fast the confession of our hope without wavering, for He who promised is faithful.
>
> Hebrews 10: 19-23

Many falter in their faith journeys, wandering aimlessly in search of solutions that evade them. These wrong and desperate attempts to seek the face of God further messes up our relationship with Him. Rather than seek for miracles, we should realize that we are the miracles that the world is waiting for (Romans 8:19).

Knowing His Ways

The knowledge of how God conducts His affairs shapes our relationship with Him. The more we know God, the closer we are to Him and the more we know His ways. It is impossible to know God's ways through our human ingenuity of observation, interrogation, or reasoning. God reveals Himself to us through intimate, sometimes, face-to-face dealings with Him. God's ways are incomprehensible and past finding out (Romans 11:33-36).

We are able to seek an intimate knowledge of God because He has chosen to reveal Himself to us. We should appreciate His sovereignty at all times.

> "3Call to Me, and I will answer you, and show you great and mighty things, which you do not know.

> Jeremiah 33:3

Familiarity with the voice of God will also help us to differentiate His ways from those of the devil. Though used interchangeably, the voice of God is distinguishable from the word of God. The latter refers to the written and the spoken word, while the voice of God refers to the words that proceed from God's mouth.

That being said, we can effectively conclude that the ways of God can be known from the voice of God, which can, in turn, be identified from having an intimate knowledge of God, through His word.

Failing to seek the ways of God makes us prey to the devil, exposing us to evils and troubles we otherwise would have avoided.

The Israelites witnessed God's deeds but failed to grasp His ways, thereby forfeiting their inheritance. Trust hinges upon knowledge, hence, we must transition from merely knowing about God to intimately knowing Him through an unwavering commitment to His word.

The Knowledge Gap

God attributes destruction to a knowledge gap and not the devil, as many believe. A lack of knowledge of the word of God puts us in vulnerable positions of lack, fear, deprivation, and incapacitation.

> "[6]My people are destroyed for lack of knowledge. Because you have rejected knowledge, I will also reject you from being priest for me."
>
> Hosea 4:6

Africans usually hold it that demons, witches, and ancestral spirits are to be held accountable for all their misfortunes. This is a cowardly and an irresponsible position to take. While some unfortunate situations are be occasioned by the devil, responsible people should not pass the buck. They know they have a part to play and they play it! While at that, they face the devil head on.

The devil cannot have a foothold in our lives when we give ourselves to knowledge, especially Biblical knowledge. It engenders peace and counteracts all the lies of the enemy (Ephesians 4:13-15).

Apostle John, in John 8:32 informs us that we will not be destroyed when we embrace the word of God. Freedom is lack of bondage and bondage is synonymous with destruction.

When we embrace knowledge, as exemplified by the scriptures, our lives become a testament to His transformative power.

Divine Revelation

We will receive divine revelation in our pursuit of intimate knowledge of God. What is divine revelation? It is an act of God occasioned by Him to bring everlasting goodness to our lives. It can be initiated by having an intimate knowledge of God, through an in-depth study of His word. By His spirit, we are brought to a deep understanding of His word. It comes alive to us and the words leap from the pages of the Bible into our hearts.

The written word of God is known as *logos*, while the revealed one is known as *Rhema*. It is possible to seek God's knowledge without the privilege of revelation. The intelligence to apply God's word follows the receiving of divine revelation.

> "¹The Revelation of Jesus Christ, which God
> gave unto him, to shew unto his servants things
> which must shortly come to pass; and he sent
> and signified it by his angel unto his servant
> John: ²Who bare record of the word of God, and
> of the testimony of Jesus Christ, and of all
> things that he saw.
>
> Revelation 1:1-2

In our pursuit, we encounter the transformative power of divine revelation. Higher than intellectual understanding, it is a sacred unveiling of truth that penetrates the depths of our souls. It redefines our perceptions and illuminates our path (Ephesians 3:18-21).

Divine revelation empowers us to embrace truth and not simply what is true. "Truth" an is absolute entity while "True" is subject to change. God's Word, is the truth and it never changes. Truth is always true, but what is true may not necessarily be the truth.

Our journey of pursuing an intimate knowledge of God should not only be restricted to the pages of the Bible. It should be a living, breathing testament to the ongoing work of God in our lives. With each passing moment, He reveals Himself afresh, inviting us into deeper communion with Him.

Pursuit Challenges

The pursuit of knowledge is not without its challenges. Along the way, we will encounter obstacles and adversaries seeking to obstruct our progress. We will find that, more than ever, the devil seeks to distract us from spending quality time with God. Yet, armed with the same word of God that the devil seeks to derail us from, we are able to press on.

> "[35]Who shall separate us from the love of Christ? Shall tribulation, or distress, or persecution, or famine, or nakedness, or peril, or sword? [36]As it is written: "For Your sake we are killed all day long; We are accounted as sheep for the slaughter." [37]Yet in all these things we are more than conquerors through Him who loved us. [38]For I am persuaded that neither death nor life, nor angels nor principalities nor powers, nor things present nor things to come, [39]nor height nor depth, nor any other created thing, shall be able to separate us from the love of God which is in Christ Jesus our Lord.
>
> Romans 8:35-39

Some of the challenges of pursuing an intimate knowledge of God are unbelief, fear, and criticism.

In an ever-changing world, defined by uncertainties, we should anchor our faith on the one who calls us to pursue Him – the unchanging God. His promises are our refuge, His presence our strength, and His love our guiding light.

The depths of divine revelation are unfathomable, and the treasures therein are inexhaustible. It takes us on a transformative journey that we will never be able to recover from. These experiences mark our lives and continue to impact our relationship with God and people. They are not meant to be one-time occurrences.

CHAPTER 2

THE BEDROCK OF REVELATION

Jesus Christ knew that the depth and strength of our faith lies in the revelation we have of Him. This is the singular factor that determines how we live. When the word of God marks our hearts, it marks our actions. Very easily one can determine a Christian who will go far and the one who will not. The revelation of the word of God has always been the separating line (John 8:32).

We cannot claim to know the word of God when we lack a revelation of it. A revelation of the word of God brings understanding. With understanding comes the ability to reproduce our word-induced experiences, time and time again. This is so because understood concepts are more likely to be retained in our minds.

In Matthew 16, we see that Jesus' position was that knowing Him is the anchor that secures us, especially in times of trials and temptations.

Whom say you that I am?

The significance of this question and the answer to it was not lost to Jesus Christ. He was known to ask deep and probing questions. I imagine His penetrating gaze compelled His disciples to rise to the occasion. His teaching style was to provide adequate understanding to His disciples. This explains why He preferred to give illustrations rather than simply offer definitions.

> "¹³When Jesus came into the coasts of caesarea Phillippi, he said to his disciples, saying whom do men say that I the son of man am? ¹⁴And they said, some say that thou art John the Baptist: some Elias: and others; Jeremias, or one of the prophets. ¹⁵He saith unto them, But whom say ye that I am? ¹⁶And Simon Peter answered and said, thou art the Christ, the son of the Living God. ¹⁷And Jesus answered and said unto him. Blessed art thou, Simon Barjona for flesh and blood hath not revealed it unto thee, but my father which is in Heaven. ¹⁸And I say also unto thee that thou art Peter and upon this rock, I will build my church; and the gates of hell shall not prevail against it. ¹⁹And I will give unto thee the keys to the kingdom of heaven: and whatsoever thou shall loose on earth shall be loosed in heaven.
>
> Matthew 16:13-19

Jesus knew that the possibility existed for his disciples to have a wrong notion of Him. This prompted Him to ask them this soul-searching question. He knew that having a correct knowledge of Him would favorably determine the quality and quantity of their discipleship efforts. An outright misrepresentation of Him, Jesus knew, would put them in a very vulnerable spiritual position. The lack of knowledge of who Jesus is, is the reason many people are still unsaved today.

Jesus Christ, the Savior and the only begotten son of God was offered as a gift to a dying world. The passionate plea to you, if you have not already done so, is to accept Him as master over your life (Romans 10:9-11). This is the escape route from the eternal judgement that is reserved for every child of disobedience.

Jesus Christ, at that time, concerned himself only with His disciples. He knew that the baton of Christianity would spread from them to the entire world. It was important, therefore, that they knew who He was. If they did not have an understanding of who Jesus Christ was, the quality of Christianity they passed to us would have been substandard.

Knowing who He is will settle your worries, anxieties, and fears. You will be able to trust the God of heaven for all your needs.

The Church of Christ is built on a solid rock

The church of Jesus is built upon the solid rock of the revelation of who Christ is. Some hold the view that the rock is Peter, which is translated *Petros* or rock. This has no basis in scripture. The choice of this revelation coming through Peter, could have been to entrench the teaching through the use of puns. A pun is a play on words – The name 'Peter' also means a rock. The practical and relational way Jesus Christ taught His lessons is revealed here.

If the church of the living God were built on Peter, it would have ended with him. It is built on the revealed knowledge of God, which exists in layers. Like an onion, one layer exposes another one. Apostle John, the favorite disciple of

Jesus Christ received a most profound revelation of Jesus Christ from God.

> "⁷Behold, he cometh with clouds; and every eye shall see him, and they also which pierced him: and all kindreds of the earth shall wail because of him. Even so, Amen. ⁸ I am Alpha and Omega, the beginning and the ending, saith the Lord, which is, and which was, and which is to come, the Almighty.⁹I John, who also am your brother, and companion in tribulation, and in the kingdom and patience of Jesus Christ, was in the isle that is called Patmos, for the word of God, and for the testimony of Jesus Christ.
>
> Revelation1:7-9

We see from the above verses that Jesus Christ is the Alpha and Omega, the beginning and the ending. This, of course, includes everything in between. We have the advantage of hind sight, insight and foresight. The first affords us a revelation of our history. Insight shows us how to navigate this terrain, and foresight points to where we are headed. We are unlike unbelievers, whose eyes are darkened and have no understanding whatsoever of what life is really all about.

There is no bias yet there is

Knowing God is not dependent on race, age, or sex. God will reveal Himself to anyone who will take the pain to seek Him. He is no respecter of persons.

> "³⁴Then Peter opened his mouth and said: "In truth I perceive that God shows no partiality. ³⁵ But in every nation whoever fears Him and

<blockquote>
works righteousness is accepted by Him.[36] The
word which God sent to the [l]children of Israel,
preaching peace through Jesus Christ—He is
Lord of all— [37]that word you know, which was
proclaimed throughout all Judea, and began
from Galilee after the baptism which John
preached. -Acts 10:34-37.
</blockquote>

Paradoxically too, He is also a respecter of persons, in that He embraces only those who come to Him. God will not force Himself on anybody. He waits for you to make a choice for Him.

The conversations around God discriminating in the administration of His mercy is ongoing. Why would He boldly declare that He would show mercy to only those He chose (Romans 9:14-18). That means, if He *chose* not to choose you, you are out! What an unrighteous and unfair God, you would say?

The Bible is not capable of private interpretation and we have a better grasp of the word of God when we compare scriptures. So, the answer to this mind-bogging question lies in the beatitudes listed in Matthew 5, verse 7 precisely. We qualify for God's mercy when we are merciful to others. We can position ourselves to receive His mercy.

The progressive knowledge of God

The more you know God, the more you realize that you do not know Him and the more you want to know Him. Our knowledge of Him will not be complete until we transition to glory.

<blockquote>
"[18]But the path of the just is like the shining sun,
That shines ever brighter unto the perfect day. [19]
</blockquote>

The way of the wicked is like darkness; They do
not know what makes them stumble."
Proverbs 4:18-19

The more we advance in our knowledge of God, the more inadequate we feel. Knowing Him exposes our insecurities. Standing before God will induce a holy fear in us. Like Moses, in the burning bush encounter, we will hide our faces from Him, for fear to look upon Him (Exodus 3:6). God dwells in the midst of unapproachable light.

We cannot do business with God if you are self-assured. We are sternly warned in the Bible that God resists the proud and honors the humble (James 4:6). To be resisted by God is to be doomed! God delights in those who need Him desperately.

Perhaps you are going through turbulent times and feel like throwing in the towel. Look here! You are still in that dark place because you are yet to receive a revelation from the word of God. You are unable to determine the next step to take because you lack insight. Now, you know what to do. Ask God to illuminate your heart and give you a revelation from His word. The Bible is not an ordinary book because it houses the power of God. So, do not read it like one.

We are the church of the living God

God is building His church on His revealed word and we are the church He is referring to. The structure of our Christian faith is laid on this solid rock. Exciting days lay ahead for the body of Christ despite the pervasive incidents of the latter days. Unknown to many, the latter days are not only about times of stress (2 Timothy 3:1). Regrettably, the negative component of the last days is the narrative many people are familiar with. The last days also promises to be a refreshing and victorious time for believers.

> "¹The word that Isaiah the son of Amoz saw concerning Judah and Jerusalem. ²Now it shall come to pass in the latter days that the mountain of the Lord's house shall be established on the top of the mountains, and shall be exalted above the hills; and all nations shall flow to it. ³Many people shall come and say, "Come, and let us go up to the mountain of the Lord, To the house of the God of Jacob; He will teach us His ways, and we shall walk in His paths." For out of Zion shall go forth the law, And the word of the Lord from Jerusalem." -Isaiah 2:1-3

These verses are repeated in Malachi 4: 1-2 for emphasis. God expects that as we round off the system of things in the world today, His word will be generously shared with His people and the world alike. This is the only way we can be the end-time church. In preparation for this great move, I received a commandment from God thus, "hearken diligently to my word".

I know that my obedience to this commandment will establish my position as a member of His end-time army. God is not a task master who issues out commands to oppress us. He demands our obedience so that He can show us off to the world.

CHAPTER 3

FROM CHILDHOOD TO SONSHIP

It is expected that every believer will transition from the state of spiritual infancy into the full stature of sonship. Our new life in Christ, regardless of age, achievement, and status, commences with us as spiritual babies (1 Peter 2:2). This stage is not expected to be permanent because the spiritual baby is not proficient with the use of the word of God. As a result, he is unable to lay hold on the promises of God. He is governed by his physical senses and lives to serve his own purposes.

Progressively increasing in the knowledge of God, will cause us to move on to maturity (Matthew 4:19). The injunction in 2 Peter 3:18 underscores the need for believers to continually grow in the grace and knowledge of our Lord and Savior, Jesus Christ.

The grace of God, as expounded in the book of Romans is not a license to sin (Romans 6:2). Rather, it is a divine enablement to live according to God's blue print for our lives. Although Christians can and have misappropriated God's grace, the opportunity for renewal and restoration is available.

Pressing On

Christians are admonished to press forward in their journey of faith, leaving behind the constraints of the past and embracing the upward call of God (Philippians 3:13). Like Jesus Christ progressed from childhood to sonship, believers are called to ascend to higher realms of spiritual authority. The distinction between Jesus' life as a child and a son, as elucidated in Luke's gospel, emphasizes the importance of maturity in fulfilling one's divine purpose.

The manifestation of God's authority in Jesus's life occurred at the time of His transfiguration. There, God publicly endorsed his ministry. This could aptly be translated as His time of maturity.

> "³⁵And a voice came out of the cloud, saying,
> "This is my beloved Son. Hear Him!""

Luke 9:35

Heirs do not have access to their inheritance until they attain the age of maturity (Ephesians 2:6). This is usually at 18 years. The world is eagerly waiting for believers who have come of age and are making their impact felt in the circles they travel. (Romans 8:19).

A deepening intimacy with God produces a willingness to embrace the responsibilities of spiritual maturity. As heirs of God's kingdom, believers are entrusted with the privilege of ushering in God's reign on earth.

A Mind Shift

The call to sonship will necessitate a departure from the old ways of doing things. The mind, which is the seat of our emotions and intellect, has to be reconfigured with the word of God.

> "²And do not be conformed to this world, but be
> transformed by the renewing of your mind, that

you may prove what is that good and acceptable
and perfect will of God.

Romans 12:2

The transition from childhood to sonship requires a mind shift, from self-centeredness to a kingdom-focused mindset. We need to move past our fears and limitations to embrace our identity in Christ.

Like the Israelites were called to possess their earthly inheritance, believers are tasked with the responsibility of advancing the kingdom of God on earth (Matthew 6:33). This necessitates a commitment to spiritual growth and a willingness to engage in the attendant spiritual battles. The pressures of life, though unpalatable, are agents of spiritual growth (James 1:2-4).

Secured in His authority

God released His power to grant us victory over the manipulations of the enemy. His authority represents His endorsement or stamp of approval on us. Having security in God terminates fears, anxieties, and establishes our victory on earth. We, no longer subject to the whims and caprices of the devil, have the courage to live offensively. The best way to defend ourselves is to live after this order.

"¹⁰See, I have this day set thee over the nations
and over the kingdoms to root out and to pull
down, and to destroy, and to throw down, to
build and to plant."

Jeremiah 1:10

The keys to unlock that ugly situation in your life are in your exercising the authority you have in Christ Jesus. Your duty is to exert dominion over all the works of the devil in your affairs - academics, family, business, and finance (1 John 3:7-8). If you refuse to do this, the devil will make a mess of your life. You should never be deceived to think that you can negotiate with the devil. Discussions with him invite compromise because he will twist God's word to play mind games on you (Genesis3:1-24). In this situation, you are unlikely to win.

You should be next to God in the order of hierarchy over your life. God will not impose Himself on you. No human, no matter how highly placed can determine the course of events of your life. Of course, the devil cannot control you unless you give Him power to. You have what it takes to establish what you desire in your life. Death and life are in the power of your tongue, so use it to your advantage (Proverbs 18:21).

Sonship in God's kingdom is born out of maturity

"Now I say, that the heir, as long as he is a child, differeth nothing from a servant, though he be lord of all." - Galatians 4:1

This verse encapsulates a profound spiritual truth about sonship in God's kingdom, highlighting the transition from immaturity to maturity, and its significance in stepping into the fullness of our inheritance as children of God.

In the natural world, an heir, though destined to inherit vast riches and authority, cannot lay hold of his inheritance as long as he remains a child. His lack of maturity prevents him from understanding, appreciating, and managing the weight of the responsibility tied to his birthright. Though he is the rightful lord of all, his immaturity keeps him in a position no different from a servant.

Similarly, in God's kingdom, sonship is not merely a matter of birthright; it is born out of spiritual maturity. While every believer is an heir of God through faith in Christ, it is spiritual growth—our deepening relationship with God, understanding of His will, and alignment with His purpose—that elevates us from mere children to mature sons and daughters who can fully embrace and walk in the authority, power, and blessings of the kingdom.

Maturity brings with it the capacity to steward God's promises effectively. A spiritually immature believer might be "lord of all" in principle, but without growth, they remain limited, unable to access the fullness of what God has made available. True sonship, therefore, is not just about belonging to God's family, but about growing into a place of authority, wisdom, and responsibility that reflects God's nature on the earth.

Sonship, born out of maturity, is a call to grow into the likeness of Christ, to embrace our spiritual inheritance not as servants who are bound by limitations, but as mature heirs who carry the weight of God's glory and kingdom on earth.

It is through maturity that we can truly say, as Christ did, "I must be about my Father's business."

CHAPTER 4

EMBRACING GOD'S WORD

The Word of God offers profound insights and guidance to navigate life successfully. It is the bedrock of our faith. The keys to unlock divine wisdom and experience perpetual victory on earth are enshrined in it. God has graciously bestowed His Word to us as the primary pathway to knowing Him (2 Timothy 3:16).

Neglecting the word of God leads to spiritual stagnation and defeat. In a world rife with false teachings, adhering to the principles outlined in scripture is necessary. Many Christian suffer from word deficiency. They do not regularly take in adequate doses of the word of God. As a result, their spirits are lean and they are susceptible to the deceit of false prophets and the allure of empty doctrines. (2 Timothy 4:3).

False doctrine is destructive, deceptive, and divisive. Christian leaders should be intentional about delivering sound doctrine to the people of God. By so doing, Christians, especially young ones, are able to identify and stand up to the manipulations of the enemy (Psalm 119:11)

The king's Word

The Word of God serves as a lamp unto our feet and a light unto our path. It illuminates darkness and eradicates confusion by providing clarity and direction.

> "[108]Accept, I pray, the freewill offerings of my
> mouth, O Lord, and teach me Your

judgments. [109]My life is continually in my hand,
Yet I do not forget Your law.

Psalm 119:108 -109

In times of uncertainty, our unwavering trust in His promises should be our source of strength. We need His word in successful times too, because it helps us to have the right perspective of ourselves and the situation.

We are able to walk in humility when we embrace the word of God (James 4:10). Pride, like lack of knowledge, destroys an it is of the devil. The panacea for pride is the word of God.

In the face of the devil, the king's word remains powerful, strong, and unyielding. The Bible is replete with instances where the word of God brought about miraculous deliverance and provision for His children.

From the shores of Galilee, to the wilderness of Judea, the word delivered life into barren situations and unleashed abundance where there was lack (Luke 5:4-9). We are positioned to receive divine favor and breakthroughs, when we align ourselves with the word of God.

What is faith?

The Bible is not merely a collection of historical events and stories. It is the book of faith that holds the very essence of God himself. To do business with God, we must cultivate a heart of faith. Our lives are displeasing to God without it.

> "[5]By faith Enoch was taken away so that he did
> not see death, "and was not found, because God
> had taken him"; for before he was taken he had
> this testimony, that he pleased God. [6]But

without faith it is impossible to please Him, for
he who comes to God must believe that He is,
and that He is a rewarder of those who diligently
seek Him.

Hebrews 11: 5-6

Verse 1 defines faith as the substance of things hoped for and the evidence of things not seen. Although most teachings focus on the unseen component of faith, it is helpful for us to bring up the 'seen' aspect of it as well. The 'substance' and 'evidence' referred to are nature, history, and archeological proofs. They are the visible components of faith.

Apologetics is the rational and physical defense of religious beliefs. As we live in an increasingly skeptical world, it is an excellent way to deepen peoples' faith. It is also a useful tool to share the gospel of Christ. Many peoples' inability to accept Christ is because they are uncertain that He truly walked on the face of this earth.

So, seeing is believing and believing is seeing.

Acting out Faith

Faith without action is futile. If we do not take any action on what we claim to believe, then we do not truly have faith. We do not act on the word of God because we do not truly believe that God is faithful.

> "[17]Thus also faith by itself, if it does not have works, is dead.[18]But someone will say, "You have faith, and I have works." Show me your faith without your works, and I will show you my faith by [b]my works. [19] You believe that

there is one God. You do well. Even the demons
believe—and tremble! [20]But do you want to
know, O foolish man, that faith without works is
[c]dead? [21]Was not Abraham our father justified
by works when he offered Isaac his son on the
altar? [22] Do you see that faith was working
together with his works, and by works faith was
made perfect?

James 2:17-22

The faithfulness of God and our faith in Him should propel us to act in accordance to His statutes. Acting out our faith should be a way of life, rather than a means to an end. We should not only take action on the word of God when we are believing Him for specific miracles of healing, provision, or deliverance.

God commands us to walk in righteousness, love our neighbors as ourselves, and pursue holiness in all our endeavors (Matthew 22:39). These are all actions of faith and we should carry them out consistently. Living in this manner shows that we are diligent seekers of God. The diligent seeker will be rewarded (Hebrews 11:6).

My Prayer Life

One of the outcomes of embracing the word of God is a thriving prayer life. When our prayer lives are powered by the word of God, we are drawn into deeper communion with God. Prayer is a communication tool with God and it enables us to align our hearts with His purposes.

"[23]Search me, O God, and know my heart; Try me,
and know my anxieties; [24]And see if there is any

wicked way in me, and lead me in the way everlasting."

Psalm 139:23-24

When we fervently seek His face in prayers, we are positioned to experience His power. Prayer should not be a monologue. It should be a dialogue between a father and His child. It is a sacred exchange between the creator and His children.

Communication with God takes place when we are reading His word, meditating upon it, talking to God, evangelizing, or discussing about God. The Bible records that God take notes when children of God talk about Him (Malachi 3:16-18). You should expect to hear from God anytime you communicate with Him. God's silence is usually an indication that something is not right. He may be silent if He has issued a command and you are refusing to carry it out (John 7:17). This may also happen if you are asking Him questions He has already provided answers to.

While we can garner prayer support when we are going through tough times, we are usually in the best position to pray for ourselves. Many people go to God to complain and murmur instead of praying. This is unacceptable. If you do not change your situation through prayers, your situation will change you. This will not be for the better, I can assure you!

CHAPTER 5

KNOWING GOD PERSONALLY

To know God personally is to see the outcomes of His word in the world around us. Through His works in creation, we see objectively that He exists. A thriving Christian life is an indication that we hold a personal knowledge of God. In the first instance, we are called to a personal relationship with God, so there is no reason not to pursue it.

Man, by nature, is a social being (Psalm 68:6) He longs to forge meaningful relationships with others. A personal quest for the supernatural beckons him to seek to know a supreme being. This life-defining activity is not a cerebral exercise. It is a spiritual journey that takes us closer to an intimate relationship with the creator of the universe. This never-ending journey continues until we get to eternity.

The longing of my heart

Deep within us lies a longing for something beyond this material world. We hold a yearning for meaning and purpose that transcends the temporal. This is as a result of an inherent need for a connection with the divine.

> "[1]As the deer pants for streams of water, so my
> soul pants for you, my God."
>
> Psalm 42:1

Just as a thirsty deer seeks water to quench its thirst, so should the human soul yearn for the presence of God to satisfy its deepest longings. It is not unusual, to find people, as they get older, wanting more meaning out of their lives. This may build a restlessness that is difficult or impossible to quell.

In our quest to know God personally, we must first acknowledge and embrace the stirrings of our hearts. Without doing this, the next steps will hardly be taken. The force in our hearts propels us to the path of spiritual discovery. As we surrender to this divine longing, we open ourselves up to a world of infinite possibilities (Ecclesiastes 3:11). The longings of our hearts is to embrace the endless possibilities that our new life in Christ offers us.

Definitive Moments

A definitive moment is a meeting with God, designed by Him, to give His children a most profound experience. It is also known as a divine encounter. Even if it were not dramatic in nature, it would still be a divine encounter. It is the moment in time when God reveals Himself to His Children in unforgettable ways.

The faith walk is facilitated by divine encounters. Moses' burning bush experience, Paul's encounter with God on the road to Damascus, and Jesus' contact with the woman with the issue of blood were pivotal moments for these patriarchs of faith. Their relationship with God was redefined.

"[20]And suddenly, a woman who had a flow of
blood for twelve years came from behind and
touched the hem of His garment. [21] For she said

> to herself, "If only I may touch His garment, I
> shall be made well." ²²But Jesus turned around,
> and when He saw her He said, "Be of good
> cheer, daughter; your faith has made you well."
> And the woman was made well from that hour."
>
> Matthew 9:20-22

Like the woman with the issue of blood, we should prepare ourselves for these encounters. She called herself to a meeting and determined to make contact with the power of God. Without a doubt, she was a woman of faith. To prepare for and make the most of our definitive moments, we must remain sensitive in the spirit.

These encounters bring us face to face with the reality of God's presence (1 Chronicles 29:11). They show His love, grace, and power in ways that defy human comprehension.

Solitude is not loneliness

In a fast-paced and noisy world, finding moments of solitude is precious. Solitude is a healthy practice that allows us to self–reflect while loneliness is a state of sadness caused by lack of company. It is often in the quietness of our hearts that we encounter the presence of God most profoundly.

> "¹⁰Be still, and know that I am God; I will be
> exalted among the nations, I will be exalted in
> the earth! ¹¹The Lord of hosts is with us; The
> God of Jacob is our refuge. Selah
>
> Psalm 46:10-11

In spite of life's chaos, confusion, distractions, and complexities, we are called to cultivate a quiet spirit to allow us to hear from God. Times of solitude may be God's way of preparing us for the next level of our lives. He may choose to do a new thing altogether. Also, he may ask us to commence a fast in order to make us more receptive to His biddings.

Our internal environment is conducive for the spirit of God, when it is regulated by the word of God. It determines the outcome of our lives (Matthew 12:34).

The Holy Spirit, also known as the comforter, offers us peace (John14:26-27).

Oh, I surrender!

The proof of love is surrender. Claiming to love someone, without surrendering to them is merely a display of rhetoric. It is like attempting to practice faith without corresponding actions (James 2:17). Talk, as they say is cheap. We must be willing to let go of our pre-conceived notions and open ourselves up to the transformative power of God's love.

> "[7]Therefore submit to God. Resist the devil and he will flee from you. [8]Draw near to God and He will draw near to you. Cleanse your hands, you sinners; and purify your hearts, you double-minded. [9]Lament and mourn and weep! Let your laughter be turned to mourning and your joy to gloom. [10] Humble yourselves in the sight of the Lord, and He will lift you up."

> James 4:7-8

God identifies with surrendered vessels because it shows Him that He is important to such people. They are assets to His kingdom and He is very keen to do business with them. God finds their willingness to be used for His glory exciting. It is in the surrendering of our hearts that we become vessels of God's love. His grace can thereby flow through us into the world around us (Luke 9:23).

Struggling with God is a sign of pride. It makes our lives hard. By so doing, we are saying that we can manage our affairs and have no need of His help. When we surrender our ways to God, we will enjoy His favor in unimaginable dimensions (Isaiah 1:19).

Hand in Hand

A good friendship is a very special gift. Typically, friends look out for one another, and share their joys and sorrows. Some characteristics of a true friendship are love, empathy, and loyalty. Based on his words in John 15:15, we can tell that Jesus Christ had a good relationship with His disciples.

> "15I no longer call you servants, because a
> servant does not know his master's business.
> Instead, I have called you friends, for everything
> that I learned from my Father I have made
> known to you."

He had a good relationship with God too. Otherwise, He would not have been able to learn so much from His father. He made all these known to His disciples.

We must develop an intimate relationship with God. One that is marked by the ingredients of a deep and abiding relationship - trust and mutual understanding (Proverbs 18:24).

In His Presence

To know a person, we must spend time in their presence. The more time we spend with people, the more we know them. Ultimately, the essence of knowing God personally lies in the joy of His presence.

> "[11]You make known to me the path of life; you
> will fill me with joy in your presence, with
> eternal pleasures at your right hand."
>
> Psalm 16:11

In God's presence, we find true fulfillment, a satisfaction that transcends the fleeting pleasures of this world. It is in knowing Him intimately that we discover the true meaning of life—a communion with the one who created us for His glory.

Irrespective of our spiritual activities, we must routinely seek to have protected or quiet times with our creator (Psalm 62:5). A personal devotion is a time that is set apart to be alone with God. Although we carry His presence with us all the time (Psalm 139:7-12), having these private moments with God helps us to know Him more personally.

CHAPTER 6

KNOWING GOD INTIMATELY

Intimacy is the hallmark of all close relationships. It connotes a willingness to open ourselves up to our beloved, which is often at the risk of being vulnerable. Peoples' unwillingness to be vulnerable with others is borne out of the fear of possible victimization. While this is understandable, it unnecessary in our dealings with God. We are assured of God's everlasting and unconditional love (Jeremiah 31:3).

Another element of intimacy is a hunger for the presence of the one we love. Most people, if not all, desire to love and be loved in the deepest way possible. An intimate knowledge of God will afford us this opportunity. When we continually seek to know God, we will be intimate with Him (James 4:8). Closeness to God means that He is our first thought when we wake up and the last before we sleep.

Beyond the Veil

The veil was a physical barrier from the presence of a holy God. Any attempt to break through it meant death for the violator (Numbers 18:7). Cerebral knowledge of God merely satisfies the intellect and keeps the veil in place. It does not hold the power to draw us, past the limitations of this world, into the presence of God.

God thoughtfully designed a pathway to make this possible. Now, we can move beyond the veil into His majestic presence on the strength of the blood of the lamb.

> "[14]how much more shall the blood of Christ, who
> through the eternal Spirit offered Himself

without spot to God, cleanse your conscience
from dead works to serve the living God? [15]And
for this reason He is the Mediator of the new
covenant, by means of death, for the redemption
of the transgressions under the first covenant,
that those who are called may receive the
promise of the eternal inheritance.

Hebrews 9:14-15

We need a new thing when the old one has developed a problem or has ceased to function. The new covenant, though a continuation of the old, is significantly different from the old one. It is also better than it (Hebrews 8:6).

The blood of Jesus Christ affords us the privilege of coming into God's presence without reservations. Under it, the Holy Spirit empowers us to carry out God's commandments (Philippians 2:13). The old covenant is harsh, forbidding, and restrictive. It commands us to obey God without any help whatsoever. It is a lifeless dispensation of 'dos' and 'don'ts.'

Heart to Heart

A person becomes intimate with another person when they hold deep and authentic conversations. The closest couples are the communicating ones. It has been discovered that people usually fall in love with those they are able to open up to. Intimacy with God is cultivated through this process of heartfelt exchanges. Our deepest desires, fears, and struggles are laid bare before Him.

"[8]Trust in him at all times, O people; pour out
your heart before him; God is a refuge for us."

Psalm 62:8

Our heavenly father would neither take advantage of our vulnerability nor condemn us. His deep and abiding love for us forbids Him to hurt us (Psalm 136:1).

In our moments of vulnerability, we discover the beauty of communing with our Heavenly Father. The beauty of intimacy with God is that He communicates back to us because He enjoys our presence. As our hearts beat as one, we can hear Him clearly and go on to do His bidding (Proverbs 23:26).

Partner Dancing

Partner dances are coordinated dance steps of two dancers only. Life is a sacred dance with our creator, with our efforts aligned with the help of the Holy Spirit. It is a profound and intricate interplay of joys and sorrows, triumphs and trials.

In our journey of intimacy with God, we are called to partner with Him in the affairs of our lives. Partnering with God is the best collaborative effort anyone could ever engage in. The word of God details the terms of engagement and there is no room for abuse.

> "[5]Who then is Paul, and who is Apollos, but ministers through whom you believed, as the Lord gave to each one? [6]I planted, Apollos watered, but God gave the increase. [7]So then neither he who plants is anything, nor he who waters, but God who gives the increase. [8]Now he who plants and he who waters are one, and each one will receive his own reward according to his own labor.

> 1 Corinthians 3:5-6

Partnering with God is a deeply fulfilling and rewarding exercise. Unlike many natural partnerships, especially those without a contractual agreement, it is for mutual benefit. We and the kingdom of God are the better for it.

Refusing to partner with God, however, has grave consequences. Even if we were religiously active people, we become spiritually barren when we refuse to collaborate with God.

Spiritual barrenness glorifies the devil (Romans 8:6-11). So, all Christians should strive to live to glorify God.

The Humanity-divinity Gap

Gaps are spaces or openings in the middle of something or between two things. They exist in knowledge, relationships, procedures and have the propensity to compromise the best efforts of people. Gaps, which are largely undesirable, always beckon to be filled.

The gap between humanity and divinity is timeless. It was created following of the fall of man in the garden of Eden (Genesis 3). God never wanted any chasm between Him and man so He bridged it through the sacrificial death of Jesus Christ.

> "⁵For there is one God, and there is one
> mediator between God and men, the man
> Christ Jesus, ⁶who gave himself as a ransom
> for all."
>
> 1 Timothy 2:5-6

The humanity-divinity gap is closed because we are created in the image and likeness of God (Genesis 1:26). This means that we carry God's characteristics and can relate with Him as our father. This life exchanges empower us to be in dominion on earth. As a result, we have the capacity to make the world a better place.

Indeed, man has done so. Today, scientific and technological innovations exist that were unheard of centuries ago.

Oneness with God

When you are one with another person, you are united with them in every way. God's marital purpose is oneness of a man and his wife in all aspects of life. Unity of the spirit is attainable when a couple are both children God.

The marriage union is a symbolism of the relationship between Christ and the Church. The Bible describes this union and the relationship between Christ and His church as a mystery (Ephesians 5:31-32). Jesus spoke about His oneness with the father.

> "[23]I in them and you in me, that they may
> become perfectly one, so that the world may
> know that you sent me and loved them even as
> you loved me."
>
> John 17:23

This profound prayer reveals the intimacy of the relationship between Christ and His followers. It is a union of souls that transcends human understanding. As we abide in Christ and

He in us, we experience a oneness with God that fulfills the deepest longings of our hearts.

Unity and disunity are unmistakable. Sometimes, though, they present themselves in the nuances of our everyday lives.

The way we conduct our affairs, our confession, and disposition to situations will announce to the world whether or not we are one with God.

The Life-long nature of intimacy with God

Intimacy with God is not a one-time event but a lifelong journey of nurturing a deep and spiritual connection. It is a journey marked by moments of joys and sorrows. Intimacy with God can be experienced in both instances.

> "[8]Oh, taste and see that the Lord is good; Blessed is the man who trusts in Him![9] Oh, fear the Lord, you His saints! There is no want to those who fear Him. [10]The young lions lack and suffer hunger; But those who seek the Lord shall not lack any good thing."
>
> Psalm 34:8-10

Intimacy is intentionally cultivated in the daily disciplines of prayer, meditation, and worship. Our knowledge of God should be a continuous exercise. No one has the capacity to know God fully on this side of the divide (1 Corinthians 13:9).

Intimacy with God eradicates fear because we know He has our backs all the time. Intimacy initiates godly fear, which is a deep and abiding reverence for God.

As Christians, the more we know of Him, the less we know. The less we know of Him, the more we want to know Him. This paradoxical aspect of God does not make him elusive, though. He reveals Himself to as many as desire to know Him, through nature and all His creation. Nature is known in theological terms to be a form of general revelation of God.

CHAPTER 7

KNOWING GOD EXPERIENTIALLY

For faith to be effectual, our belief in God should transcend mere intellectual assent. Mentally assenting to God cannot be translated to mean a renewal of the mind (Romans 12:1-3). This is possible only through the agency of the word of God. Our knowledge of God is concretized when we experience Him (Psalm 34:8). Experience, whether ours or those of others, is a good teacher. Without it, our faith remains in the abstract realm. The word of God is the best teacher anyone can have.

In moments of encounter, revelation, and divine intervention that we come to truly know God in the depths of our souls. This journey is marked by encounters that eternally transform us - moments of divine presence, recognition of God's providence in every situation, and understanding His messages through the language of the heart.

Divine Encounters

Whether divine or not, life is full of defining moments - when we experience something that radically changes the way we think and behave. Divine encounters are orchestrated by God. From the unexpected whisper in the stillness of prayer to the miraculous intervention in the midst of chaos, these encounters leave an indelible mark on our souls. We are forever changed for the better.

> "²⁴ Then Jacob was left alone; and a Man wrestled with him until the breaking of day. ²⁵Now when He saw that He did not prevail against him, He touched the socket of his hip; and the socket of Jacob's hip was out of joint as He wrestled with him. ²⁶And He said, "Let Me go, for the day breaks." But he said, "I will not let You go unless You bless me!" ²⁷ So He said to him, "What is your name?" He said, "Jacob." ²⁸And He said, "Your name shall no longer be called Jacob, but Israel; for you have struggled with God and with men, and have prevailed."
>
> Genesis 32:24-32

Divine encounters do not happen to anybody or everybody. Only those who are prepared experience His power. We must habitually position ourselves for God's visitation. He is sovereign and does what He wills, when He wills, and how He wills (Colossians 1:16-17). Our duty is to wait on Him.

Divine encounters leave us indebted to God forever, leaving impressions that shape our relationship with God. Our faith walk will lack zest, be shallow and rigid if we do not experience divine encounters.

Speechless Before Him

In a catastrophic and complex world, finding moments of silence can be a rare and precious gift. Yet, it is in the silence of our hearts that we often encounter the presence of God most profoundly.

"¹Keep silence before Me, O coastlands, and let
the people renew their strength! Let them come
near, then let them speak; Let us come near
together for judgment. ²"Who raised up one
from the east? Who in righteousness called him
to His feet? Who gave the nations before him,
and made him rule over kings? Who gave them
as the dust to his sword, as driven stubble to his
bow?

Isaiah 41:1-2

In the stillness of our souls, we can hear the voice of God speaking to us, guiding us, and comforting us with His presence.

Silence in God's presence may mean that we hold Him in deep regard. Much more than we want to hear ourselves, we want to hear what He has to say to us. It is in this mode that we can behold His majesty.

The impact of an event may leave us speechless. Excitement, sadness, anger are all emotions that have the tendency to take our voice away.

The Unseen Hand

Although we cannot see God, the works of His hands are evident all around us. Our world shows us the creativity and glory of God. This is clear from nature to technological and scientific innovations.

God's providence is also evident in the way He orchestrates the events of our lives. Children of God will always have the last laugh over the devil. Many of us find Joseph's 'from prison to palace' experience in Genesis 37-50 very touching. However, we may not perform so well, should we find ourselves in his desperate situation.

> "[1]Now Joseph had been taken down to Egypt. And Potiphar, an officer of Pharaoh, captain of the guard, an Egyptian, bought him from the Ishmaelites who had taken him down there. [2]The Lord was with Joseph, and he was a successful man; and he was in the house of his master the Egyptian.[3] And his master saw that the Lord was with him and that the Lord made all he did to prosper in his hand. [4]So Joseph found favor in his sight, and served him. Then he made him overseer of his house, and all that he had he put under his authority."
>
> Genesis 39:1-4

It is said that we live life forwards but understand it backwards. It takes time for us to have a full understanding of the intervention of God in our lives. In times of stress, we are usually blinded to God's activities in our lives.

Joseph, however, did not live in this manner. He recognized God's hand in His life at every point. He could see how God orchestrated the events of his life for a greater purpose.

In the same way, we should trust in God's providence, knowing that He works all things together for our good (Romans 8:28). We should never allow the devil to frustrate us or convince us that God does not care when we are going through turbulent seasons.

Proclaiming the good news

Experiencing God's love should necessitate us to proclaim the good news. Evangelism offers the opportunity for people to experience the life-transforming power of Christ. Merely showing compassion to an unsaved person will not secure his eternal destiny. We should carry out our acts of kindness on the strength of our experiential knowledge of God.

> "[18]Go therefore and make disciples of all nations, baptizing them in the name of the Father and of the Son and of the Holy Spirit, [19]teaching them to observe all that I have commanded you."
>
> Matthew 28:19-20

Through evangelism and discipleship, we should share our kingdom experiences to encourage people. Evangelism brings people into the kingdom of God, while discipleship efforts keeps them firmly there. Its goal is to make disciples of men, who will, in turn, make disciples of others (Matthew 4:19).

The Great Commission (Matthew 28:19-20) does not only refer to evangelism, as many think. Really, many of our evangelism efforts are not with people that we know or have regular contact with. How then is it possible, as indicated in the above scripture to 'teach prospective converts to observe all that Jesus Christ commanded his disciples? Evidently, this is discipleship, because it is possible only with people in our regular circles.

CHAPTER 8
KNOWING GOD THROUGH THE WORD

In our ever-changing world, navigating through the life can be daunting and finding direction is proving to be more challenging by the day. As such people resort to self- help and quick fixes in an attempt to proffer solutions to their challenges. At such times, they will not do business with the word of God.

Neglecting the word of God will ultimately lead to disobedience. In extreme cases, it may lead to an outright rejection of God (2 Peter 2:17).

The word of God stands as a balefire of truth and guidance. It is a source of wisdom and revelation that illuminates our path and deepens our understanding of God (Psalm 119:105). The word of God remains the veritable channel through which we get to know Him. This journey, marked by the discovery of His voice, is a 'must embark on' for every believer.

Hearing God's voice in His word

The voice of God are the words that proceed directly from the mouth of God. His word, on the other hand, is the written and revealed word of God, known as the *logos* and *Rhema* respectively. The Bible is more than just a collection of ancient writings. It is the Word of God and it is backed up by His power.

Our adeptness at using the word of God will empower us to identify His voice. On a daily basis, we hear different voices – God's, the devil's, the world's, and ours.

> "[14]But if you have bitter envy and self-seeking in your hearts, do not boast and lie against the truth. [15]This wisdom does not descend from above, but is earthly, sensual, demonic. [16]For where envy and self-seeking exist, confusion and every evil thing are there. [17]But the wisdom that is from above is first pure, then peaceable, gentle, willing to yield, full of mercy and good fruits, without partiality and without hypocrisy."
>
> James 3:14-17

If we are not in the habit of administering God's word to our situations, we will get confused and ultimately be deceived. Interestingly, the devil can say God's word right back to us. (Matthew 4:) If we are unable to identify his voice we will be swayed off course.

Through the pages of scripture, we encounter the voice of God speaking to us, guiding us, and revealing His mind to us. It is incumbent on us to know how to recognize His voice.

The path of wisdom

The word of God is the primary supplier of wisdom to the people of God. The Bible is replete with timeless principles that guide us along life's journey.

"⁵Trust in the Lord with all your heart and lean
not on your own understanding; ⁶in all your
ways submit to him, and he will make your
paths straight"

Proverbs 3:5-6

Wisdom can be derived from various sources – God, the devil, the world, and self (James 3:16-17). We must be spiritually intelligent enough to tell them apart. Otherwise, we will get into trouble time and time again. Self is one of the worst leaders of man.

Through the study and application of God's Word, we are equipped to navigate life's challenges with wisdom and grace, trusting in God's guidance and provision every step of the way.

Mind Transformation

A transformed mind is one that has been cultured and textured by the word of God. When the word of God is sustainably introduced to the mind, the resulting effect is transformation. The natural disposition of man is to rebel against God. A transformed man has the capacity to submit to the will of God.

"¹I beseech you therefore, brethren, by the
mercies of God, that you present your bodies a
living sacrifice, holy, acceptable to God, which
is your reasonable service. ²And do not be
conformed to this world, but be transformed by
the renewing of your mind, that you may prove
what is that good and acceptable and perfect will
of God."

Romans 12:1-2

Knowing the will of God is not a mysterious concept. It is basically accessible through the knowledge of the word of God. We must sustainably and consistently feed on the word of God (Psalm 36:8). Only then can His will be known to us.

Some people erroneously think they can pray their way into the will of God. Although we can ask God to lead us to His will, we will not know it until we know His mind. His word is His mind. It is the compass that will direct order your steps in His pre-arranged direction.

The treasures hunt

The treasure hunt is a favorite game of children, usually within the ages of 3 and 8 years of age. It a time-sensitive game with clues to search for hidden objects. The Bible is a treasure trove of riches waiting to be uncovered by children of God.

> "[162]I rejoice at Your word as one who finds great treasure."
>
> Psalm 119:162

Without a doubt, the treasures embedded in the word of God can be discovered in Psalm 119, among other scriptures. Every verse of its 176 verses talk about the word of God. Synonyms like precepts, statutes, laws, judgements, and commandments are used throughout the chapter to describe God's word.

Just as children are excited when they discover hidden treasures, we too, like David, should rejoice upon our discovery of the word of God (Psalm 119:174).

Through the study and exploration of scripture, we discover hidden gems of wisdom, revelation, and insight that enrich our lives and deepen our understanding of God and His purposes.

Taking steps in truth

The ultimate goal of knowing God is to apply the knowledge that we acquire. Although knowledge is powerful, failing to apply what we know is as bad as not having acquired it in the first place.

> "22Do not merely listen to the word, and so
> deceive yourselves. Do what it says.
>
> James 1:22

We walk in the light of the word of God when we apply it to all areas of our lives. No part of our lives should escape the search light of His word. The more we apply the word of God to our situations, the better we get at the process. Our proficiency with the word of God improves with use. This principle of use applies in all spheres of life.

Applying God's word to our situations also makes us better teachers and mentors. Applied knowledge can be more readily passed on to others. Attempting to teach what we have not applied may prove to be a very difficult task. In the event that we succeeded in teaching it well, the power of God will hardly back up such an exercise. This could very well be described as hypocrisy (Matthew 23:27-28).

Struggling to teach will certainly not produce understanding, neither for the student nor the teacher (1 John 1:1).

Knowing to do exploits

There is a relationship between seeking God and living (Amos 5:4-6). The quality of your life is directly proportional to how well you know God. You will know God more by seeking Him. 'Live' means living out the plan of God for your life. Only those who know their God are really living and are the ones who will do exploits for Him.

> "32Those who do wickedly against the covenant
> he shall corrupt with flattery; but the people who
> know their God shall be strong, and carry out
> great exploits.
>
> Daniel 11:32

The spirit is to God what the flesh is to the devil. We are only able to interact with God with our spirits. This is why carnal people cannot know God (1 Corinthians 2:14-16). Their inability and unwillingness to gain ascendancy in the things of the spirit cuts them off from knowing God.

CHAPTER 9

MANIFESTING THE GLORY OF GOD

We learnt in the previous chapter that we get more proficient with the word of God as we use it. In the same way, the more we know God, the more we experience His manifest glory. Although God is omnipresent, He does not manifest His glory everywhere. Being intentional about our relationship with Christ guarantees the experience of His glory.

God's fullness can be translated to mean the glory of God (Colossians 2:9-10). This is the totality of everything God is. That is why we sometimes talk about the weight of His glory.

To know God personally is to live in His presence. His holy presence affords us the privilege of experiencing his wisdom, might, and love. The resulting effect of this is our transformation. No one comes in contact with God and remains the same. The transformative power of the Holy Spirit changes us as He moves in our midst.

Mirroring God in our daily lives

God calls us to reflect His attributes of love, mercy, compassion, justice, and righteousness in our daily lives. When we hold the fullness of God, by reason of an incremental knowledge of Him, we cannot but reflect His image. Man will ultimately manifest what he is full of.

"³⁴For out of the abundance of the heart the
mouth speaks. A good man out of the good
treasure of his heart brings forth good things,
and an evil man out of the evil treasure brings
forth evil things.

Matthew 12:34

It will be evident to others whether or not we have trapped the glory of God by the actions we take, the words we speak, and decisions we make.

God is very intentional about the matters of His kingdom. As such, He will not share His glory with an unyielding and disobedient vessel. Manifesting His glory or putting God on display is the essence of our salvation in the first place.

We are living epistles

Unbelievers get their perception of God through us. As a matter of fact, many people, Christians inclusive, 'read' believers more than they do the Bible. Mahatma Gandhi said, "I like your Christ, but not your Christianity. Your Christians are so unlike your Christ" It would appear that Mahatma, at least, had some knowledge about Christ. He knew what to expect. Even then he had a negative perception of Christians. This should not be so.

We are expected to project Jesus Christ all the time.

"²You yourselves are our letter, written on our
hearts, known and read by everyone. ³You show
that you are a letter from Christ, the result of our
ministry, written not with ink but with the Spirit
of the living God, not on tablets of stone but on
tablets of human hearts.

2 Corinthians 3:2-3

We are more likely to influence people when our lives are testimonies of God's compassion. This is the concept of relational evangelism. In it, Christians make friends with unbelievers with the intention of winning them to Christ on the strength of their friendship. Christianity without compassion is not Christianity at all. In the same way, unfriendly Christians are not imitators of Christ. *He* was friendly, uncondemning and accommodating (Mark 2:15).

We are shining lights

Our world is in a state of crisis. The tensions keep rising with spiraling food and energy costs, escalating wars, global warming, and signs of environmental collapse. People are overwhelmed by the darkness that threatens to take over the world (Micah 3). Jesus Christ is very clear about our role in the world.

> "[14]You are the light of the world. A town built on a hill cannot be hidden. [15]Neither do people light a lamp and put it under a bowl. Instead they put it on its stand, and it gives light to everyone in the house. [16]In the same way, let your light shine before others, that they may see your good deeds and glorify your Father in heaven."
>
> Matthew 5:14-16

The church of the living God has been and remains a major provider of social services. Good social services profoundly affect the quality of life of citizens.

We shine our light to the world when we get involved in our communities by doing acts of kindness like organizing community libraries, food banks, medical, and educational support.

My role as a change driver

Our place as children of God affords us the opportunity to be transformed into a new man by the indwelling presence of the Holy Spirit. What this means is that the transformative power of the Holy Spirit is at work in our mortal bodies. (Romans 8:11). God's power is not available in us for our benefit alone. We should collaborate with God to transform peoples' lives by preaching the gospel, praying for the sick, and administering deliverance to the oppressed.

> "[1]The Spirit of the Lord God is upon me; because the Lord hath anointed me to preach good tidings unto the meek; he hath sent me to bind up the brokenhearted, to proclaim liberty to the captives, and the opening of the prison to them that are bound; [2]To proclaim the acceptable year of the Lord, and the day of vengeance of our God; to comfort all that mourn.

Isaiah 61:1-2

We can drive everlasting change in the lives of people when we preach to gospel of Christ. People responding to the call of God and the work they subsequently do for Him are the only aspects of their lives that speak in eternity.

Through the power of His Spirit working within us, we become agents of transformation by participating in God's work of renewal and restoration in the world.

CHAPTER 10

FROM SERVANTHOOD TO SONSHIP

As children of God, we must understand our role as heirs of God's kingdom. Having the knowledge of who we are in Christ is a confidence booster. It gives us the wherewithal to hold our own in the world. Unbelievers, understandably, are unsure of their identity. It is particularly sobering when Christians also share this experience. Inability to discern our status in Christ is a sign of spiritual immaturity.

The devil will ride roughshod over Christians in this category. He lacks the capacity to consider anyone's feelings. His primary objective is to steal and destroy everything that God has blessed us with (John 10:10).

Lack of knowledge makes us vulnerable to the enemy. Through the abiding presence of the Holy Spirit, we can be sure of who we are in Christ (Galatians 4:7).

Embracing Sonship in God's family

Following our salvation, we need to undergo a mind shift to accept our new-found freedom in Christ. Our new ranking grants us the privilege to become beloved children of God. Our mind shift tool is the knowledge of God.

It is a privilege to be called children of God. A particular religious affiliation would rather be called servants of God. I guess, from a false sense of humility. Although we are called to serve God and one another, we are called to see ourselves the way God sees us (John 15:15).

Through the sacrificial love of Jesus Christ, we are adopted into God's family, welcomed with open arms, and invited into an intimate relationship with the Father.

Free at last!

Freedom in Christ guarantees our release from of sin and death (Galatians 5:1). Living in bondage to the enemy can be a very traumatic experience. His victims stumble through life, trying to make meaning out of it. More often than not, they make wrong decisions. Sustaining this unhealthy practice will ultimately lead to a derailment from destiny and possibly eternal damnation.

The good news is that we are free from the bondage of the enemy! We are free to live our best lives now!

The devil constantly accuses and intimidates children of God. By afflicting us with low self-esteem, he causes us to doubt the love of God for us (John 10:10). Through the indwelling presence of the Holy Spirit, however, we are empowered to overcome these negative emotions and experience the love of God (2 Timothy 1:7).

Inheritance of grace

According to Ephesians 1:4-14, our inheritance in Christ includes being chosen in Christ, our predestination as His sons and daughters through Jesus Christ, redemption through Christ's blood, the forgiveness of sins, and the knowledge of the His will.

> "[3]Praise be to the God and Father of our Lord Jesus Christ! In his great mercy he has given us new birth into a living hope through the resurrection of Jesus Christ from the dead, [4]and into an inheritance that can never perish, spoil or fade.
>
> 1 Peter 1:3-4

Our inheritance includes not only the riches of His grace and mercy but also the assurance of eternal life and the privilege of being co-heirs with Christ.

My father's love

A father's roles include mentoring, encouragement, and comfort. His physical presence around the home makes his children to feel safe and protected. If natural fathers can offer this level of security, how much more can our heavenly father do? God's love is unwavering and He desires His children to know, trust, and love Him as a father.

It is held that mothers are not designed to give this level of security. They also draw security from their husbands. The Bible clearly states that the man is the spiritual leader and head of the household (1 Corinthians 11:3). In most climes, children carry the names of their fathers.

> "[3]But I want you to know that the head of every
> man is Christ, the head of woman is man, and
> the head of Christ is God."

God's love remains steadfast and unwavering. Even when we err (Luke 15:11-32), He lovingly looks out for us and awaits our return. His ever-waiting arms eagerly wait to hold us close. In the Father's love, we find the warmth of acceptance and the security of belonging to His family.

Prayers for peace

Prayer, which is broadly defined as communication with God, is earthly permission for heavenly intervention. This could be in our lives, other peoples,' communities, territories, and nations. Mature Christians understand the need to pray for their countries.

> "[1]Therefore, I exhort first of all that
> supplications, prayers, intercessions, and giving
> of thanks be made for all men, [2]for kings and all
> who are in authority, that we may lead a quiet
> and peaceable life in all godliness and
> reverence. [3]For this is good and acceptable in
> the sight of God our Savior, 4who desires all
> men to be saved and to come to the knowledge
> of the truth."

1 Timothy 2:1-3

Global environmental issues of overpopulation, climate change, and global warming are at an all-time high. Government after government is working feverishly to keep these issues in check. Things, however, keep spiraling out of control.

Our role is to pray for all people, including those in positions of authority, in our countries. This engenders peaceful living and cohabitation. Failing to heed this call, makes life difficult for the citizens.

Although Christians operate under the covenant of exemption (Psalm 92), they will, in one way or the other, be affected by the laws that govern the place of their habitation. They will not be left out of prevailing situations in the society.

An instance that comes readily to mind is the emergence of the COVID-19 pandemic. The economic and social disruptions caused by it affected Christians and non-Christians alike.

The importance of praying for our leaders and countries cannot be overemphasized. The ruling class are the ones who determine the tone, traditions, norms, and culture of our societies.

CHAPTER 11

MANIFESTING THE FULLNESS OF GOD

The more we know God, the more we will experience His fullness in our lives. Colossians 2:9 informs us that we have been brought to fullness in Christ. This means that the knowledge of God brings us to fullness or a state of completion. Being complete in Jesus is to be made whole, soul, mind, and body. The Bible informs us that Christ has done all that needed to be done for us (2 Peter 1:3).

Everything that touches the spiritual and natural components of our lives have been accounted for. Nothing was missing, broken, or left out. We therefore have no reason to be an emotional mess, struggle to make ends meet, or live unfulfilling lives.

Christians must be able to draw the line between their natural and spiritual lives. An intelligent interplay of the two will afford us the benefit of manifesting God's fullness in our lives. Our inability to do this will cause us to fall short of God's best for our lives.

The natural image versus the divine one

Humanity was originally created in the image and likeness of God. They were thus created to show off the excellency of their maker. No other being was created in this wise.

"²⁷So God created mankind in his own image, in
the image of God he created them; male and
female he created them.
Genesis 1:27

The sin of man, however, distorted this image. It tarnished his ability to fully reflect God's glory. Through the advent of Christ, we are restored to our original purpose—to manifest the fullness of God's glory in human form.

The Holy Spirit is the agency for our conformity to the image of God. He speaks the mind of God to us, strengthens us in our times of weakness, and scolds us if need be. All His efforts are geared towards making us better Christians. Without Him, we will remain helpless and unable to perform our God-ordained role to the world.

God's abundance

Abundance is the state of having more than enough. God does not want His children to merely survive. Rather, He wants them to experience abundance in all areas of their lives. This is the order that supports the fullness of Christ.

Hardly can we be a blessing to others when we are struggling to make ends meet. We are more likely to influence others when our lives reflect God's goodness.

God's abundance, however, is not limited to material things alone (Romans 14:17-20). It covers all aspects of our lives: spiritual, social, educational, and relationship (marital and otherwise).

"¹⁰The thief does not come except to steal, and to
kill, and to destroy. I have come that they may

<blockquote>
have life, and that they may have it more
abundantly. [11]I am the good shepherd. The good
shepherd gives His life for the sheep.
</blockquote>

John 10: 10-11

The ministry of the devil is to subvert the purpose of Christ. He is all out to destroy the glorious plans that God has for us. (John 10:10). This explains why Jesus Christ wants us to be alert at all times. Letting down our guard can have grave consequences. The devil will usually strike us in our vulnerable moments and when we are isolated from other people, Christians in particular.

Walking in power and authority

God makes power available to His children to grant them victory over the enemy. We cannot claim to be experiencing the fullness of God when the enemy beats us black and blue. God's authority, which is a sign of His approval, is an indication of His fullness. As children of God, we are entrusted with the mandate of representing God's kingdom on earth.

<blockquote>
"[18]All authority in heaven and on earth has been
given to me. [19]Therefore. go and make disciples
of all nations, baptizing them in the name of the
Father and of the Son and of the Holy Spirit,
[20]and teaching them to obey everything I have
commanded you."
</blockquote>

Matthew 28:18-20.

The scripture above highlights what God expects of His children. Being a fair and just God, He will not give us responsibilities without the attendant power and authority to carry them out.

Power without authority is frustrating and authority without power is humiliating. The fullness of life in Christ offers us both.

We do not need to occupy positions of authority to hold sway in God's kingdom. Power and authority are available to every believer upon their naturalization as citizens of the kingdom of God (Matthew 28:18-20).

Fullness in obedience

It is impossible to experience the fullness of God in a state of disobedience. God will not release His abundance to hard-hearted people. Hardheartedness is a sign of pride and God is adamantly opposed to proud people (James 4:6). To manifest the fullness of God, we must be willing to surrender our will, desires, and ambitions to His perfect plan.

> "[26]I will give you a new heart and put a new
> spirit within you; I will take the heart of stone
> out of your flesh and give you a heart of flesh. [27]
> I will put My Spirit within you and cause you to
> walk in My statutes, and you will keep My
> judgments and do them."
>
> Ezekiel 26:26-27

The word of God is the mind-softening agent that helps us to cultivate a teachable spirit. We experience a mind renewal when continually fill our minds with it (Colossians 3:16). The fullness of God will be our experience when we allow God's word to dwell richly in us.

Dispensers of God's grace

Believers who have benefitted of the grace of God should willingly dispense it. Taking without giving, like in the natural sense, is a sign of selfishness. Humans and animals excrete what they consume. When they are stuffed with food, they may feel bloated or nauseous. Excretion takes place to support a functioning digestive system. Belching is a way of releasing excess air from the upper digestive tract.

As recipients of God's grace, we should release His blessing to those around us.

> "And God is able to bless you abundantly, so
> that in all things at all times, having all that you
> need, you will abound in every good work."
>
> 2 Corinthians 9:8

In the same manner that God lavished His grace upon us, we are expected to extend the same to others. We should seek to use our financial and material resources to meet their physical and spiritual needs. The former is comprised of food, shelter, clothing etc. while the latter covers healings, restoration, deliverance etc.

Our societies suffer when we and even non-Christians refuse to give back. One of the indicators of fine citizens is their willingness to make a positive difference in their societies.

These actions are expressions of God's fullness in the lives of His Children.

However, the good deeds of unbelievers are immaterial to God (Isaiah 64:6-7).

CHAPTER 12
BELIEVING HIS WORD

Faith in is the currency of heaven. It forms the basis of our experiences in the kingdom of God. Being the foundational principle that underpins our entire spiritual quest, our Christian life is meaningless without it. This chapter takes us through transformative power inherent in believing God's Word. It sheds light on how glorious our lives can be when we choose to please God by living a life of faith (Hebrews 11:6).

It is only by the consistent hearing or ingesting of the word of God that we can acquire or grow our faith. To some, faith is a mysterious phenomenon. For reasons unknown to them, it has eluded them, despite their efforts to read their Bibles and attend religious activities.

To acquire faith, ingesting the word of God has to be a way of life (Romans 10:17). It has to be done in and out of season. This way, God's word will find a resting place in our hearts to yield the desired results.

Child-like faith

Although our spiritual maturity is an all-important issue to God, there is a child-like quality to our walk with Him. Children are trusting, eager, forgiving, and simple. God endorses these attitudes and expects us to emulate them all the time.

> "15Truly, I say to you, whoever does not receive the kingdom of God like a child shall not enter it.
>
> Mark 10:15

As children of faith, we should embrace God's word with simplicity and allow it to take root in us. A seed, when nurtured, grows into a mighty oak. In the same way, the seed of faith, when watered by the word, burgeons into a towering tree of faith. Questioning God's word is a sign of rudeness, arrogance, and pride. This does not mean, however, that we cannot ask God well-intentioned questions (Isaiah 1:18).

Our spiritual maturity is directly proportional to our child-likeness. Although this sounds contradictory, it is the way of the spirit (Luke 18:17). The manner of the natural man and the spiritual one are significantly different (1 Corinthians 2:14-16). The former is unable to accept the things of God, while the latter has a keen understanding of it. It is his pleasure to prosecute them.

The servant's posture

The Bible enjoins servants to obey their masters in all things. This may involve the giving up of dreams and aspirations to serve their purposes.

> "[9]Exhort bondservants to be obedient to their
> own masters, to be well pleasing in all things,
> not answering back, [10]not pilfering, but showing
> all good fidelity, that they may adorn the
> doctrine of God our Savior in all things."
>
> Titus 2:9-10

This is usually not an easy thing to do. For one, people hold their dreams dear and nurture them with the hope of realizing them one day. Another reason is that some masters, because of the position of authority they occupy, are hostile and overbearing to their servants. Remaining loyal under such stressful situations is possible only by the grace of God (Ephesians 6:1).

We should be willing to give up our dreams and aspirations for the cause of the gospel, if necessary. This is achievable when we allow the word of God to regulate our lives. People who have done so never had any reason to regret their actions. On the contrary, they experienced a quality of life much better than the one they were holding on to (Genesis 26:12).

Sonship and Inheritance

Heirs have access to their inheritance when they attain the age of maturity, usually 18. In the same way, our spiritual inheritance is only available to us when attain spiritual maturity.

> "[3]His divine power has granted to us all things
> that pertain to life and godliness, through the
> knowledge of him who called us to his own
> glory and excellence, [4]by which he has granted
> to us his precious and very great promises.
>
> 2 Peter 1:3-4

To get access to our inheritance, we must lay hold on it by faith. Failure to do so makes the inheritance only potentially ours, meaning we merely hold the possibility of obtaining our inheritance. It is by the correct handling of the word of God that it can be realistically and experientially ours.

The word of God clearly spells out the terms of the contract binding our inheritance. This document, if we may call it that, serves as a form of protection to the believer. It also provides guidance on how to conduct our affairs on this side of the divide and what happens thereafter.

Drawing life from the source

A Yoruba proverb says that a river that forgets its source will eventually dry up. Life and power are drawn from the word of God and maintained by staying connected to the same. Jesus Christ is the sacrificial lamb through whom we received salvation. He is our source and it is in our best interest to stay connected to Him. The Bible describes Him as the vine. We are the branches.

> "⁵I am the vine; you are the branches. Whoever
> abides in me and I in him, he it is that bears
> much fruit, for apart from me you can do
> nothing.
>
> John 15:5

As branches grafted into the vine of Christ, we are expected to witness to the transformative power of abiding in His Word. This exercise causes us to produce fruits that testify to the dealings of God in our lives. Abiding in God's word and producing fruits accordingly, go hand in hand.

Manifesting the fruit of the spirit are some of the expected outcomes of our connection to the vine (Galatians 5:22-23).

The fruit of the Spirit is love, joy, peace, patience, kindness, goodness, faithfulness, gentleness, and self-control.

Leaving a legacy of faith

Twilight years are usually times of sober reflections. Some people look back with gratitude, while others have a reason or two to regret. Committedly living a life of faith is the way to secure peace for ourselves in our later years. The acquisition of material possessions is not necessarily an indication that we have faith in God (Romans 14:17).

We should leave a legacy of our unwavering faith in God. If anything will be said of us, let it be that we remained faithful until the end.

> [20]He did not waver at the promise of God through unbelief, but was strengthened in faith, giving glory to God, [21]and being fully convinced that what He had promised He was also able to perform.
>
> Romans 4:20-21

When we pass the baton of faith to future generations, we are entrusting them with the word of God.

It behooves church leaders to enhance the capacity of future generations to administer God's estate (Psalm 78:5-8). Knowledge facilitates engagement. When Christians know what to do, it is easier for them to perform their roles.

Uncertainty and ignorance will slow us down in the pursuit of a deep knowledge of God.

CHAPTER 13

THE LOVE STORY

Most people like a good love story, with the expected happily-ever-after ending. More often than not, its characters fall in love against all odds. The love of God for man has the 'against all odds' features, in that we were sinners when Christ died for us (Romans 5:8). Most Christians, if not all, can share stories of how they resisted the tug of God on their hearts, preferring rather to follow the devil.

God's love surpasses human comprehension and defies all logic (John 3:16). It makes for the best love story ever written. Experiencing the transformative power of God's love is a most fulfilling experience. It should propel us to continually seek to reproduce God's love story in as many lives as we can.

Appreciating the love of God

When we appreciate something, it means that we are grateful for it or have an understanding of its value. The love of God is the essence of our faith walk. For many people, Christians inclusive, the love of God is incomprehensible. In a world of 'dog eat dog,' hearing that God loves us with an everlasting love, that Jesus Christ died for us while we were yet sinners, and that we are expected to love our enemies is simply too much to handle. The transformative power of the Holy Ghost makes this possible for us.

> "[18]May have strength to comprehend with all the saints what is the breadth and length and height and depth, [19]and to know the love of Christ that

surpasses knowledge, that you may be filled
with all the fullness of God."

Ephesians 3:18-19

When we consider God's love for us, our hearts should be stirred with gratitude, awe, and reverence for the One who loved us first. The best people in our lives are grossly incapable of loving us the way God does. No human has the capacity to love us unceasingly like God does (Lamentations 3:21-26).

Rejoicing in His embrace

In God's embrace, we find true love and are empowered to accept ourselves. Self- acceptance, especially in the face of past sins and guilt, can be a mentally grueling task. The devil will play mind games with us and continually deceive us that God has not forgiven us (Micah 7:19).

In His presence, however, we need not feel intimidated or insecure. His unwavering love helps us to progressively transition into the best version of our selves.

"³The Lord has appeared of old to me, saying:
"Yes, I have loved you with an everlasting love;
therefore with lovingkindness I have drawn you.
⁴ Again I will build you, and you shall be
rebuilt, O virgin of Israel! You shall again be
adorned with your tambourines, and shall go
forth in the dances of those who rejoice."

Jeremiah 31:3-4

The everlasting and unconditional nature of God's love is true to the ever-abiding nature of God himself. God is love! If He were broken into a million pieces, every piece would be love. No matter how far we stray, His loving eyes tirelessly follow us, waiting eagerly for us to make our way back home. 'Home' is in His embrace (Luke 15:20-24).

Holding on in adversity

Trials and tribulations, joys and sorrows, victories and defeats are certain life companions (John 16:33). The changing seasons of life offer us the most inexplicable joys and rough times. Although the life difficulties may threaten to overwhelm us, we are encouraged to remain strong, even in the face of adversity. The unchanging nature of God's love facilitates this process.

> "38For I am sure that neither death nor life, nor angels nor rulers, nor things present nor things to come, nor powers, 39nor height nor depth, nor anything else in all creation, will be able to separate us from the love of God in Christ Jesus our Lord"
>
> Romans 8:38-39

The cords of the love of God are so strong, that the strongest threats to the world and our personal struggles cannot separate us from the love of God. We have His assurance that His grip on us is firm and He is not about to relax His hold on us (Deuteronomy 31:6).

Christians are encouraged to stay in the love of God by remaining connected to Him. We will suffer if we fail to do this. This is why we sometimes feel lonely, depressed, and isolated. God is always faithful. We are the ones who break the terms of the agreement (2 Timothy 2:13).

The touch of His love

Our love for other people is the litmus test of our love for God. God is love and we cannot claim to love Him if we do not love others. How can we love an unseen God if we do not love a seen people?

Love and giving go together. Our call mandates us to imitate God, who is a sold-out giver? (Matthew 7:9-11). Is there anything good He would withhold from us?

> "16For God so loved the world that He gave His
> only begotten Son, that whoever believes in Him
> should not perish but have everlasting life.

John 3:16

Unbelievers and Christians alike need of the touch of God. The former does because the world is steeped in sin. As such, the devil takes advantage of their situation to make their lives unbearable. Christians need to have times of refreshing in God's presence (Acts 3:20). Still, some may have need of deliverance because they are being assaulted by the devil (2 Corinthians 7:1).

For both sets of people, God equips His children to initiate a revival. A revival is a time of awakening. Never is the touch of God more experienced than during a revival.

Compassionate action

Societal reforms usually follow a revival. During these times, man experiences the love of God so profoundly that the society is the better for it. This is shown through the showing of compassionate actions like organizing medical outreaches, opening community kitchens, speaking up for the oppressed, and the establishment of schools and hospitals.

Our bowels of compassion should be stirred when we come across the sick, the marginalized, and the downtrodden. Looking away is unbecoming for a child of God.

> "25For I was hungry and you gave me food, I was thirsty and you gave me drink, I was a stranger and you welcomed me,26 I was naked and you clothed me, I was sick and you visited me, I was in prison and you came to me.
>
> Matthew 25:35-36

Also, we cannot afford to be critical and judgmental of others. It is important that we are sympathetic and empathetic to their plight. When we are not, we push them away and this negatively projects Christ to them. This is unacceptable because our aim should be to win them to Christ. Having compassion restrains us from hurting people (2 Corinthians 5:14-19).

Showing hospitality

Christian hospitality is looking out for the needs of others. It is immaterial to us whether or not they can reciprocate our gesture. What motivates us is the love of God and the desire to bring people into the God's kingdom. Arguably, one of the most profound ways of showing hospitality is by receiving guests into our homes (Hebrews 13:2).

"⁹Be hospitable to one another without
grumbling. ¹⁰As each one has received a gift,
minister it to one another, as good stewards of
the manifold grace of God. ¹¹If anyone speaks,
let him speak as the oracles of God. If anyone
ministers, let him do it as with the ability which
God supplies, that in all things God may be
glorified through Jesus Christ, to whom belong
the glory and the dominion forever and ever.
Amen."

1 Peter 4:9-11

When we joyfully open our homes to people, we have in effect, opened our hearts to them. We cannot keep people at a distance and expect that they will be touched by the love of God.

Whether through sharing of a meal, offering a listening ear, or providing a place to rest, hospitality creates opportunities for meaningful connections and fosters a sense of community.

CHAPTER 14

KNOWING WHO WE WORSHIP

Worship is showing regard with deep devotion and respect for a deity. This could be a god, goddess, or a supreme being. Forms of it are divine worship, hero worship, self-worship, animal worship etc. Hindus believe that cows are sacred, so they worship them. Christians are commanded to worship the living God (John 4:22-24).

Worshipping God has a calming effect and renews our minds. As we continually worship the living God, we experience peace in our lives. (Isaiah 66:12-13). The peace that Jesus Christ offers passes all human understanding.

Elements of worship are singing, teaching, praying, and meditation. Christians usually relate singing to worship, thinking that the speed of songs determine if it is a praise or worship song. The slower paced songs, they believe, are worship songs. This is wrong. Although we can use songs to worship God, worship is not singing. It is the surrender of our lives to God.

Worship driven by knowledge

The depth of our worship is influenced by our understanding of the act of worship itself. Worship, as earlier indicated, is not the activity of singing. It a life style that is influenced by the knowledge of who God is and how He conducts His affairs. Life is spiritual and a lack of knowledge of this fact will incapacitate our best efforts to worship God.

> "²³But the hour cometh, and now is, when the
> true worshippers shall worship the Father in
> spirit and in truth: for the Father seeketh such to
> worship him. ²⁴God is a Spirit: and they that
> worship him must worship him in spirit and in
> truth.
>
> John 4:23-24

We cannot truly worship God, if our spirits are not alive to Him. This is because we communicate with Him through our spirits. It is the intercourse of the Holy Spirit and our spirits that drives our knowledge of God.

In worship, we are struck by the revelation of who God is and are compelled to bow our hearts before Him (Psalm 95:6-7).

The dynamics of our relationship

Our knowledge of God determines how rich or otherwise our relationship with him is. The living God is to be known, He is to be worshipped. It is impossible to truly worship an unknown God? How close can you be to God if you do not know Him too well or at all?

> "⁷Dear friends, let us love one another, for love
> comes from God. Everyone who loves has been
> born of God and knows God. ⁸Whoever does not
> love does not know God, because God is love.
>
> I John 4:7-8

God desires our relationship with Him to be founded on intimacy and knowledge, rather than empty religious observance. The knowledge of God can be deepened through prayer, study, and communion with Him. Riding on the wings of these, our relationship will transition from a distant acquaintance to a close and personal bond.

Self-perception

Our self-perception is shaped by how well we know God. Our self-esteem will receive a serious bashing if our knowledge of God is scanty. It takes spiritual insight to be able to comprehend our ranking as God's children.

> "¹⁷That the God of our Lord Jesus Christ, the
> Father of glory, may give unto you the spirit of
> wisdom and revelation in the knowledge of him:
> ¹⁸The eyes of your understanding being
> enlightened; that ye may know what is the hope
> of his calling, and what the riches of the glory of
> his inheritance in the saints"
>
> Ephesians 1:17-18

We behold the glory of God in the place of worship. It is impossible to behold the glory of God and still hold a wrong perception of ourselves (2 Corinthians 3:18). The glory of God is all-encompassing and it takes us to higher realms in our walk with God.

When the light of God floods our hearts, it is revealed to us by His spirit, that God is strong in might, All-powerful, and magnificent (Ephesians 1:18-19). Thus, our faith increases and we are empowered to believe that we are who He says we are.

Impacting the world

We pick up God's character traits when we spend time with Him. We are all products of our associations. This is true in the natural and spiritual sense. Jesus Christ is one with the father, therefore He carries His character.

When we spend time in worship and live a life style of adoration to God, His character rubs off on us. God's character is one of impact. It is no wonder we are commissioned to shine our light to the world.

> "[14]Ye are the light of the world. A city that is set on an hill cannot be hid. [15]Neither do men light a candle, and put it under a bushel, but on a candlestick; and it giveth light unto all that are in the house. [16]Let your light so shine before men, that they may see your good works, and glorify your Father which is in heaven."
>
> Matthew 5:14-16

As we begin to worship God out of knowledge, we become beacons of His light, illuminating the darkness, and pointing others to Him. Through acts of love, compassion, and service, we demonstrate the reality of God's kingdom and invite others to experience His transformative power.

Walking in the light

Light illuminates the darkness and brings every hidden thing into the open. People move around freely and are less likely to stumble when lights are on. The light of God symbolizes truth. As upholders of truth, we should strive to live transparent lives. A worshipper walks in the light of God.

> "⁵This then is the message which we have heard of him, and declare unto you, that God is light, and in him is no darkness at all. ⁶If we say that we have fellowship with him, and walk in darkness, we lie, and do not the truth: ⁷But if we walk in the light, as he is in the light, we have fellowship one with another, and the blood of Jesus Christ his Son cleanseth us from all sin."
>
> 1 John 1:5-7

Lack of transparency causes people to hide themselves or sections of their lives from others (John 3:21). What happens when people are walking in darkness is that their private and public lives are not harmonized. They are motivated to behave differently in their different life spaces.

This is more like a split personality syndrome, where people are controlled by two or more separate personalities. These are evil or demonic manifestations because such people may even report hearing voices (Matthew 4:1-11).

Even if they claimed that they were not suffering from the disorder and were not hearing voices, they cannot deny the fact that it takes a manipulation of the devil to live deceitfully (Proverbs 26:24-26). This is unacceptable for a child of God.

Walking in the light will not accommodate such a practice. It requires transparency, honesty, and a commitment to live according to His Word. It is by living in this manner that we experience true fellowship with God and one with another.

Mind Transformation

A transformed mind is one that has been cultured and textured by the word of God. The natural disposition of man is to rebel against God. A transformed man is able to know and submit to the will of God.

> "[1]I beseech you therefore, brethren, by the mercies of God, that you present your bodies a living sacrifice, holy, acceptable to God, which is your reasonable service. [2]And do not be conformed to this world, but be transformed by the renewing of your mind, that you may prove what is that good and acceptable and perfect will of God.
>
> Romans 12:1-2

A person whose mind has been transformed will have his beliefs, perceptions, attitudes, and values shaped by the word of God. He willingly takes up the humble disposition of Christ in his relationships (Philippians 2:5-11). This is God's doing and unachievable without the help of God.

It is through the exercise of mind transformation that that we will be able to prosecute the will of God for our lives. Indeed, it is this same activity that will position us to know the will of God in the first place. Our worship of God is true only when it emanates from a mind that is subjected to His will. (John 4:24).

CHAPTER 15
ALONE WITH GOD

"But Jesus often withdrew to lonely places and prayed."

— Luke 5:16 (NIV)

The Sacred Invitation

There is a deep yearning in every soul that cannot be satisfied by the world around us. We search for fulfillment in achievements, relationships, and the noise of daily life, yet still, a quiet whisper inside calls for something more, something greater. It is the call to be alone with God.

In the chaotic rhythm of our lives, solitude may seem like a luxury we cannot afford, or worse, a place of emptiness and loneliness. Yet, when we step into that sacred space of being alone with God, we find it to be the place where life truly begins. Here, in the stillness, we encounter the fullness of His love, the clarity of His voice, and the beauty of His presence. It is in these intimate moments that God invites us not only to know about Him but to truly know Him.

Jesus, our perfect example, understood this need deeply. Though surrounded by crowds, demands, and a mission that would change the course of history, He often withdrew to lonely places to pray (Luke 5:16). He knew that the strength, wisdom, and peace He needed could only be found in communion with the Father. If even the Son of God needed time alone with God, how much more do we?

In this chapter, we will explore the profound importance of solitude with God. We will look at how these sacred moments change us, refresh us, and draw us closer to the heart of our Creator. As we journey through this reflection, may we discover the beauty and power of being alone with the One who knows us better than we know ourselves.

1. The Call to Solitude: A Holy Retreat.

And it came to pass in those days that he went out into a mountain to pray, and continued all night in prayer to God. Luke 6:12.

The Bible is filled with stories of God calling His people into moments of solitude. From Moses meeting God on the mountain to Elijah hearing the whisper of God in the cave, these encounters often happened in the quiet places, far from the noise of the world. Solitude is not just a chance to escape the hustle and bustle of life; it is an invitation to retreat into the presence of the Divine. Jesus in His usual and common attitude, often goes into the mountain and prays all night.

Imagine, for a moment, the scene with Moses on Mount Sinai. He climbed that mountain alone, leaving behind the crowd of Israelites. In the stillness of that high place, he encountered the living God, who spoke to him face to face as a friend. The words Moses received in that solitary moment was what shaped the future of an entire nation while they were on their journey to the promise land.

Or consider Elijah, exhausted and afraid after fleeing for his life. He, too, found himself alone on a mountain, desperate for God's guidance. But instead of encountering God in the wind, the earthquake, or the fire, Elijah heard God in the gentle whisper (1 Kings 19:12). It was in the silence, in the absence of noise and distraction, that God's voice was clearest.

Today, God still calls us into these moments of solitude, inviting us to leave behind the distractions of life and climb our own "mountains"—whether that means stepping away from our responsibilities for a few moments or creating intentional space in our busy schedules. He invites us into the quiet places where we can hear His voice and experience His presence in a deeper way.

But solitude is more than physical isolation; it is a posture of the heart. It is about quieting the noise within, turning off the constant stream of thoughts and worries that often dominate our minds, and choosing to listen for God's still, small voice. This is the sacred retreat we are all called to—whether we are standing on a literal mountain or sitting in the corner of a busy café. God's call to solitude is a call to be with Him, to know Him, and to be transformed by His love.

2. Hearing God's Voice: The Language of Silence

"Be still, and know that I am God." (Psalm 46:10) — These words echo through the pages of Scripture, reminding us that it is in the stillness we come to know God. But in a world that values speed and productivity, being still can feel like a foreign concept. Yet, it is in these moments of stillness, when we are alone with God, that we can truly hear His voice.

Hearing God is not always about receiving grand revelations or dramatic visions. Often, it is about recognizing the quiet promptings of the Holy Spirit, the subtle nudges that guide our hearts and direct our paths. These whispers are easily missed in the chaos of life, but in the silence, they become clear.

Think of the times when you've struggled to make a decision, when your mind was swirling with options and uncertainties. It is in these moments that God gently calls you to be still. He doesn't force His voice upon you; He waits for you to quiet your heart, to turn your attention to Him. And when you do, you hear Him—not necessarily with your ears, but with your spirit. His voice may come as a deep sense of peace, a word from Scripture that resonates in your heart, or a thought that brings clarity.

But how can we cultivate this ability to hear God? It begins with creating intentional space for silence and reflection. We must be willing to lay aside our agendas and schedules, to step away from the noise of life and sit quietly before God. This can be uncomfortable at first. Our minds may race, and we may be tempted to fill the silence with our own thoughts or words. But as we learn to rest in the silence, we begin to recognize the voice of God.

Hearing God's voice is not about mastering a skill; it is about cultivating a relationship. Just as we grow to know the voice of a loved one through time spent together, we grow to know the voice of God by spending time in His presence. In the stillness, we come to understand His heart, His desires, and His will for our lives.

3. Resting in His Presence: The Healing of the Soul

In the presence of God, there is fullness of joy (Psalm 16:11). But how often do we truly rest in that presence? In our fast-paced world, rest is often seen as unproductive or lazy. We are taught to value busyness, to measure our worth by how much we accomplish. Yet, God invites us to rest in Him, to lay down our burdens and simply be in His presence.

Resting in God's presence is not about doing nothing; it is about being filled with everything we need. When we are alone with God, we are reminded that we do not have to strive for His love or approval. We are already loved, already accepted, already enough. In His presence, we can let go of the need to perform and simply rest in the knowledge that we are His beloved children.

For many of us, this kind of rest does not come naturally. We are so used to being in control, to managing our lives, that the idea of surrendering everything to God feels unsettling. But when we choose to rest in His presence, we find that He is more than capable of carrying our burdens. We find peace that surpasses understanding, a deep sense of trust in His goodness, and a renewed strength for the journey ahead.

This rest is not just physical; it is emotional, mental, and spiritual. It is the kind of rest that heals the soul. When we are alone with God, we are given the space to process our hurts, to grieve our losses, and to find comfort in His arms. We are reminded that we are not alone, that God is with us in every moment, carrying us through every storm.

Resting in God's presence is a radical act of trust. It is a declaration that we believe God is enough—that His grace is sufficient, His love is unfailing, and His promises are true. When we rest in Him, we are free to let go of our anxieties, our fears, and our need to control. We are free to simply be with Him, to enjoy His presence, and to receive the healing that only He can give.

4. Transformation Through Intimacy: Becoming More Like Christ

As we spend time alone with God, something miraculous begins to happen: we are transformed. This transformation is not the result of our own efforts but the work of the Holy Spirit within us. In the presence of God, we are changed from the inside out.

Consider the story of Jacob, who wrestled with God through the night. In that moment of intimate struggle, Jacob's life was forever altered. He walked away from that encounter with a limp, but he also walked away with a new identity—no longer Jacob the deceiver, but Israel, the one who struggled with God and prevailed. When we are alone with God, we too are given new identities. We are no longer defined by our past, our failures, or our weaknesses. We are defined by who God says we are—His children, His beloved, His chosen ones.

This transformation is not always immediate or dramatic. Often, it is a slow, steady process of being molded into the image of Christ. As we spend time in His presence, we begin to take on His character. Our desires align with His, our thoughts are renewed by His truth, and our hearts are softened by His love.

Transformation through intimacy with God is not about behavior modification; it is about heart transformation. It is about becoming more like Jesus, not by trying harder, but by abiding in Him. The more time we spend alone with God, the more we are changed. His love transforms us, His grace empowers us, and His presence sustains us.

5. The Power of Silence and Reflection: Finding God in the Stillness

We live in a world that values noise. There is always something demanding our attention, always something pulling us in a thousand different directions. But in the midst of the chaos, God calls us to be still.

In the silence, we find space to reflect on who God is and who we are in Him. We are given the opportunity to meditate on His Word, to contemplate His goodness, and to surrender our lives to His will. Silence is not empty; it is full of potential. It is in the stillness that we often encounter the deepest truths about ourselves and about God.

But silence can be uncomfortable. We are so used to filling every moment with noise that the idea of sitting in quiet reflection can feel foreign, even unsettling. Yet, it is in these moments of silence that we are most likely to hear the voice of God. When we stop striving, stop talking, and stop trying to control the outcome, we create space for God to move.

Reflection is a powerful tool in our spiritual lives. It allows us to pause and consider how God has been at work in our lives, to recognize the ways He has been faithful, and to thank Him for His goodness. In the silence, we can ask ourselves hard questions, seek God's wisdom, and listen for His guidance.

The power of silence is not just in the absence of noise but in the presence of God. It is in the quiet moments, when we are alone with Him, that we come to know Him in ways we never could in the busyness of life. Silence gives us the opportunity to slow down, to breathe, and to open our hearts to the One who is always speaking, always moving, and always loving us.

Conclusion: The Beauty of Being Alone with God

Being alone with God is not a burden; it is a gift. It is an invitation to step away from the noise of life and into the peace of His presence. In these moments of solitude, we find rest, we hear His voice, we are transformed by His love, and we experience the power of silence and reflection.

May we never take for granted the sacredness of being alone with God. May we seek these moments with intentionality and cherish them with reverence. For it is in the quiet, in the stillness, that we come to know the One who created us, loves us, and longs to be with us.

This plan offers a detailed foundation for a deeply engaging chapter that could be expanded with more scriptural references, personal stories, and practical applications to reach the 7000-word target. Would you like further elaboration on any particular section?

CHAPTER 16

THE CONCLUSION OF THE MATTER

Christians should seek to know God as this the essence of our salvation in the first place. If we desire to know God, we will know Him. We don't know God simply because we do not want to. God is not elusive and He constantly beckons at us to come into intimate fellowship with Him (Jeremiah 29: 13-14).

Even unbelievers cannot excuse their lack of knowledge of God. His person and character are revealed in the things He created. From the gentle breeze that refreshes us to frightening thunder storms and the exquisite flowers that beautify our world, they hear and 'see' God on a minutely basis (Romans 1:20).

It took a great deal of investment from God for His redemptive plan for mankind to be set in motion and established. It is rudeness, carelessness, and spiritual insensitivity to attempt to make a mockery of His efforts. Refusing to know God, whether as a believer (Jeremiah 25:7) or unbeliever (2 Thessalonians 1:8-9), has dire consequences.

At the conclusion of this transformative book on knowing God, we find ourselves at the threshold of a profound revelation that this life-changing exercise is not confined to the pages of this book or the walls of a church. Our quest should find expression in our hearts and our lives. This is the culmination of our spiritual quest and the fulfillment of our deepest longing. The reality is that knowing God intimately is the ultimate purpose for which we were created.

With a seed of faith planted in the fertile soil of our hearts, we begin to develop a child-like trust in the faithfulness of our Heavenly Father. Like a sapling, reaching out for the much-needed sunlight, this faith is nourished by the living waters of God's Word and the enablement of the Holy Spirit. Despite the trials, tribulations, joys and sorrows, encountered along the way, we came out free and victories (Romans 8:37).

Our new ranking as beloved children of God, calls us to manifest the fullness of God's glory in our lives by reflecting His image to the world. We cannot justify our knowledge of God when we fail to present Him to a lost and dying world (Matthew 28:16–20).

We saw that the journey of life should be a most profound one – marked by divine knowledge, intimate communion, experiential revelation, and transformative encounters. Our responsibility is to guide others to experience the same.

Blessings !

www.ingramcontent.com/pod-product-compliance
Lightning Source LLC
Chambersburg PA
CBHW061246140726
47998CB00006B/2117